SPORTS Machines

ATVs

By E. S. Budd

The Child's World®

Published by The Child's World®
PO Box 326
Chanhassen, MN 55317-0326
800-599-READ
www.childsworld.com

Design and Production:
The Creative Spark, San Juan Capistrano, CA

Photo Credits: Images on pages 5 and 6 © 2003 Polaris Industries. Images on
pages 9 (top), 14, and 16 © 2003 Kawasaki Motors Corp., USA. All rights
reserved. All other images © 2003 David M. Budd Photography.

Library of Congress Cataloging-in-Publication Data
Cataloging-in-Publication data for this title has been applied for and is available
from the United States Library of Congress.

Contents

Let's Ride an ATV!

All-**terrain** vehicles, or ATVs, are made for off-road action. On an ATV, riders can travel over rough roads, sand dunes, and mountain trails. They can venture into places where trucks, four-wheel drives, and other vehicles can't go. ATVs open up the wilderness for adventure and fun!

The first ATVs were built in Japan. They were used to travel in mountain areas. Japanese companies thought these vehicles could be used for recreation.

ATVs arrived in the United States in 1970. They had three wheels and small engines. Ever since, people have been using these vehicles in many ways— for fun and work. Today ATVs have four wheels and much more powerful engines. They are also safer than the early ATVs.

ATVs can travel on snow and sand without getting stuck. They can move up steep slopes at high speeds. Hunters can travel into the backcountry on ATVs. It brings out a sense of adventure—ATV riders are explorers!

Responsible ATV riders respect the environment. They share trails with hikers, cyclists, and others who enjoy nature. Responsible ATV riders leave the environment better than they found it.

ATVs are a great way for families to spend time together. People of all ages—from young children to grandparents—enjoy riding ATVs.

At first, children ride with adults. Once they learn how, they can drive an ATV by themselves. The most important thing is to take safety seriously at all times.

The right gear is the first step to safe off-road action. Helmets are the most important piece of equipment. They protect riders from serious injury. They also keep riders more comfortable in cold or windy conditions.

ATV riders wear goggles to shield their eyes. Pads for the hips, knees, elbows, chest, and back protect riders in an accident. Sturdy gloves protect the hands from hazards such as tree branches. They also give the rider a firm grip on the handlebars.

ATVs may be most popular for recreation, but some people use them in their jobs. Farmers and ranchers use ATVs to travel their land and carry supplies. Search-and-rescue teams use them to travel into the wilderness.

An ATV can be used as an ambulance in places where bigger vehicles can't go. They even help people with disabilities get around more easily.

Racing ATVs is an exciting sport for riders of every ability. ATV **motocross** races are held on closed dirt tracks. These tracks have sharp turns and rugged terrain. It's a challenging ride!

Riders of the same ability race against each other. Some enjoy drag racing to see who has the fastest vehicle. In areas with cold winters, some riders even race on ice. They don't want to wait until the next summer to ride again!

Climb Aboard!

Would you like to see what it's like to ride an ATV? Special tires provide **traction** on sand, dirt, or snow. Shock absorbers keep the ride smooth. A powerful engine allows riders to do tricks and stunts.

Up Close

ATV riders use handlebars to control their ATVs. The **throttle** and **brake** are on the handlebars. The throttle speeds up the ATV. The brake slows it down. An ATV also has a foot brake. A key operates the **ignition** switch. The starter turns on the engine once the key is turned. The engine stop switch turns off the vehicle.

1. Tires
2. Shock absorbers
3. Handlebars
4. Hand brakes
5. Footrest

6. Ignition
7. Starter
8. Stop switch
9. Throttle

Glossary

brake (BRAYK) A brake is a control on an ATV. It helps the rider stop or slow down.

ignition (ig-NISH-en) An ignition is a control on an ATV. It prepares the engine to start.

motocross (MOH-toh-cross) Motocross is a sport in which motorized vehicles are raced on a dirt course with sharp turns and jumps. Some ATV riders compete in motocross races.

posture (POS-chur) Posture is a way of positioning the body. Good posture is important on an ATV.

terrain (tuh-RAIN) Terrain is an area of land, especially its natural features. ATV stands for **a**ll-**t**errain **v**ehicle.

throttle (THRAWT-ull) A throttle is a control on an ATV. It helps riders control how fast they go.

traction (TRAK-shun) Traction is friction that helps to move a vehicle forward and keep it from sliding. The tires on an ATV provide traction.